The Sea Witch

TAPPING INTO THE POWER OF THE OCEAN AND ITS CREATURES

The Sea Witch: Tapping into the Power of the Ocean and its Creatures

Contents

Chapter 1: The Call of the Sea

The relentless waves crashing against the shore, the infinite horizon that stretches as far as the eye can see, the invigorating scent of salt in the air— these are the captivating sensations of the sea that have enthralled mankind since the dawn of time. From these sensations emerges an ancient, alluring, and profoundly magical realm: the world of sea magic.

Every culture, across continents and ages, boasts legends of the sea—tales of mermaids, krakens, and sea serpents. These stories, though varied, have one thing in common: a deep acknowledgment of the sea's power and the mysteries it holds. But among all the stories that have emerged from the ocean's depths, the tales of sea witches stand out the most, for they capture the essence of humanity's relationship with the sea—a relationship steeped in reverence, respect, and, for some, a desire to harness its power.

Historical Significance and Tales of Sea Witches

To truly understand the essence of a sea witch, one must dive deep into history and folklore. The archetype of the sea witch can be traced back to ancient civilizations. In many cultures, they were revered figures who could communicate with the spirits of the sea, predict storms, control the tides, and, most significantly, act as a bridge between our world and the magical underwater realms.

One of the earliest and most renowned tales comes from the Norse mythology—the story of Rán, the sea goddess. Rán was said to have a net with which she caught sailors who ventured too far, pulling them into her watery depths. While she might sound menacing, her role was crucial. She represented the unpredictable nature of the sea, reminding sailors of the ocean's might and the respect it commanded.

But not all tales painted sea witches or their counterparts in such formidable light. In Slavic folklore, the Rusalka—water nymphs or spirits—were often seen as benevolent entities. They were spirits of women who had met untimely ends, and in their new form, they played, sang, and danced by the water, sometimes even helping crops grow. However, if wronged, a Rusalka could turn vengeful, much like the tumultuous sea during a storm.

In more recent history, tales of sea witches found a prominent place in Scotland and the broader British Isles. They were often wise women who lived by the sea, providing guidance to sailors, dispensing herbal remedies, and occasionally casting spells, for good or ill. Their wisdom was sought, especially when journeys were to be made across the unpredictable waters. They became intermediaries between the village folk and the vast ocean.

The Unique Connection Between the Ocean and Magic

So, why has the ocean always been such a fertile ground for magic and mystery? The answer lies in its vastness, its depth, its unpredictability, and its essential nature. The sea is both a giver and taker of life. It feeds entire civilizations, provides routes for exploration and trade, and yet, in its depths and during its storms, can be unyieldingly merciless.

Magic, in many traditions, is about channeling natural energies, and few forces on Earth are as potent and raw as the sea. Water, in itself, is a primal element—associated with emotions, intuition, and the subconscious mind. The sea, with its ever-changing tides, mirrors the cyclical nature of life and the rhythms of our very existence.

Every wave that crashes on the shore is a testament to the ocean's enduring power. Each tide, influenced by the moon's pull, resonates with the subtle energies of the universe. A sea witch understands these rhythms intuitively. To them, the call of a seagull is not just a sound but a message. The patterns in which seaweed gets washed ashore is not random but a sign.

The ocean's vast expanse also serves as a reminder of the boundless possibilities and the mysteries that lie beyond our understanding. Just as we have barely scratched the surface of the ocean's depths, so too have we only begun to understand the depths of magic and our own potential.

For many, the call of the sea is irresistible. It's a call to adventure, to the unknown, to discovery. But for the sea witch, it's a call to come home, to tap into ancient power, and to weave magic that resonates with the heartbeats of the ocean.

To embark on the path of sea magic is to accept an invitation from the sea itself—an invitation to understand its depths, to respect its power, and to become one with its endless ebb and flow. The journey won't always be smooth sailing; after all, the sea is as tempestuous as it is serene. But for those who heed its call, the rewards are as vast and profound as the ocean itself.

In the chapters that follow, we will navigate this mystical realm, exploring rituals, understanding the ocean's energies, and diving deep into the tales and practices that have been passed down through generations. So, brace yourself for this voyage, for the sea awaits, and its mysteries are waiting to be unraveled.

Chapter 2: Understanding Ocean Energies

The vast ocean, covering over 70% of our Earth's surface, is a mysterious entity. Its depths hide secrets that have yet to be discovered, its shores have inspired countless poems, songs, and stories, and its energies are potent, primal, and intricately woven into the fabric of our world. As we delve into the realm of oceanic magic and sea witchery, understanding these energies becomes paramount.

The Ebbs and Flows: Ocean Currents and Tides

The rhythmic dance of the tides, as they rush towards the shore only to retreat, is a visual representation of the life force that drives the ocean. This perpetual motion, the ebb and flow, is guided by the gravitational interactions between the Earth, Moon, and Sun.

Ocean currents, on the other hand, are vast river-like flows within the ocean itself. Driven by the Earth's rotation, wind, temperature, and salinity differences, these currents play a critical role in regulating the Earth's climate and transporting heat around the globe. To the sea witch, these currents represent the underlying forces of the universe, the energies that flow beneath the surface, unseen but always present.

The tides, with their predictable yet ever-changing patterns, teach us about cycles, balance, and the delicate dance between holding on and letting go. High tide brings with it a rush of incoming energy, perfect for spells of attraction, growth, and manifestation. The ebbing low tide, conversely, symbolizes release, banishment, and cleansing. Recognizing and harnessing these tidal energies allows the sea witch to work in harmony with the natural rhythms of the ocean.

Lunar Connections: Moon Phases and Their Influence on the Ocean

No discussion about the ocean's energy would be complete without acknowledging the profound influence of the moon. Its gravitational pull is the primary driver of tides. As the moon waxes and wanes, so do the tides respond, dancing to a lunar symphony that has been played for billions of years.

The new moon, a time of darkness and introspection, coincides with neap tides – when the difference between high and low tide is minimal. It's a time of stillness, reflection, and setting new intentions. As the moon waxes towards its full phase, the tides amplify, culminating in spring tides during the full moon, where the high tides are at their highest and the low tides at their lowest. The full moon, in all its luminous glory, is a time of heightened energy, completion, and manifestation.

Understanding these lunar connections is crucial for the sea witch. By aligning rituals, spells, and intentions with the appropriate moon phase and corresponding tidal behavior, the practitioner can tap into and amplify the ocean's inherent power.

Ocean Storms and Their Powerful Energies

While the rhythmic dance of tides represents balance and cyclicity and the moon's phases symbolize the ebb and flow of energies, ocean storms embody raw, unbridled power. These tempestuous displays of nature's might can be both awe-inspiring and fearsome.

Ocean storms arise from a combination of atmospheric conditions, often involving temperature differences, wind patterns, and oceanic factors. These storms, with their roaring waves and tumultuous winds, are packed with kinetic and potential energy.

To the sea witch, these storms are more than just meteorological events. They are a representation of chaos, change, and transformation. They symbolize the challenges we face, the adversities that shake us but also have the potential to reshape and redefine our paths. Harnessing the energy of an ocean storm requires respect, caution, and understanding. It's about tapping into its immense power to fuel transformative spells, protective barriers, and even to channel its energy for healing.

In moments of calm reflection by the sea, one can hear whispers of ancient lore, feel the gentle tug of lunar energies, and sense the impending power of a brewing storm. By understanding these energies - the currents, the tides, the moon's influence, and the fierce power of oceanic tempests - the practitioner is better equipped to navigate the deep waters of sea witchery, to become one with the ocean, and to tap into its boundless magic.

In the chapters that follow, we will explore how to align with these energies, incorporate them into rituals, and weave them into the very essence of our magical practices. The ocean, with its depths and mysteries, beckons. Will you heed its call?

Chapter 3: Sea Symbols and Sigils

The vast expanse of the ocean, with its ever-changing tides and unexplored depths, has been a reservoir of mysticism and wonder for millennia. The sea's treasures, from the tiniest grain of sand to the grandeur of coral reefs, are not only mesmerizing to look at but are also embedded with symbols that hold profound magical significance. These symbols, intertwined with the energies of the ocean, form the foundation of sea magic.

Decoding Symbols of the Deep: Shells, Corals, and Other Ocean Treasures

Every item that the ocean touches becomes imbued with its energy, making sea relics powerful tools for magic. Let's dive deeper into understanding these symbols:

Shells: These natural wonders are perhaps the most iconic representatives of the sea. Each shell, with its unique pattern, size, and color, is a testament to the diversity of marine life. Spirals often found on shells symbolize the never-ending circle of life, growth, and evolution. For example, the conch shell, with its intricate design and expansive cavity, is often associated with the divine feminine and the voice of the goddess. Its trumpet-like sound is believed to announce the divine presence.

Corals: These living organisms, which often resemble plants, are the backbone of marine ecosystems. Their intricate patterns speak of resilience, growth, and community. Red coral, with its vibrant hue, is often associated with passion, strength, and transformation. On the other hand, white coral symbolizes purity, peace, and spiritual enlightenment.

Seaweed and Kelp: Draped across ocean rocks or floating freely in the water, seaweed and kelp are symbols of adaptability and flow. Their long, waving tendrils remind us of the importance of being flexible and moving with life's currents.

Sea Glass: These are shards of glass that the sea has polished over time, turning them into smooth, frosted gems. Sea glass symbolizes transformation—how the rough edges of life can be smoothed over time, yielding beauty in adversity.

Driftwood: Carried by ocean currents from one shore to another, driftwood epitomizes the journey of life. Its rugged appearance speaks of survival, endurance, and the wisdom gained from experience.

Crafting Your Own Sea Sigils

While nature offers us symbols ready for use, crafting your own sigils adds a personal touch and a direct link to your intentions. Sigils are symbols charged with specific intentions, and when crafted correctly, they can be powerful catalysts for sea magic.

Here's a simple guide to crafting your own sea sigil:

State Your Intention: Begin by clearly defining what you wish to manifest. It could be anything from finding inner peace to seeking protection during sea rituals.

Condense Your Intention: Write down your intention and then eliminate any vowels and duplicate consonants. This will leave you with a string of unique letters.

Design Your Sigil: Using the remaining letters, start designing your sigil. You can incorporate shapes reminiscent of the sea, like waves, spirals, or crescent moons. Remember, it doesn't have to be perfect—what matters is the intention behind it.

Charge Your Sigil: Once your sigil is ready, it's time to charge it with energy. Sit by the sea, holding the sigil in your hand, and visualize your intention flowing into it. You can also place it under the moonlight or bury it in the sand to tap into the ocean's energy.

Activate and Use: Once charged, your sigil is ready for use. You can carve it onto candles, draw it on your body, or even inscribe it on pieces of sea glass or driftwood. Whenever you see or touch the sigil, remember the power and intention behind it.

The Importance of Symbolism in Sea Magic

Symbols have been an integral part of human consciousness since time immemorial. They transcend languages and speak directly to our souls, evoking emotions, memories, and connections. In sea magic, symbols act as bridges between the physical and metaphysical realms.

Here's why symbolism is pivotal in sea magic:

Universal Language: Whether you're invoking the protection of sea deities or seeking to enhance your intuition, symbols provide a universal language that resonates with both the practitioner and the forces being invoked.

Amplifying Intentions: Just as a magnifying glass focuses sunlight, symbols concentrate and amplify our intentions. A simple shell, when used with intent, can become a powerful tool for divination or protection.

Connectivity: Symbols, especially those from the sea, remind us of our interconnectedness. Using them in rituals helps us tap into the collective consciousness of all beings influenced by the ocean.

Anchoring Energy: Symbols act as anchors, grounding our energy and ensuring that our rituals and spells are firmly rooted in our intentions and the energies of the ocean.

Aiding Visualization: For many practitioners, visualizing intentions can be challenging. Symbols, with their direct representation, provide a focal point, making visualization more accessible and potent.

The sea, with its myriad treasures, offers a vast palette of symbols waiting to be decoded and harnessed. Whether you're drawn to the spiral of a shell or the rugged endurance of driftwood, each symbol carries a story, a lesson, and a magical potential. By understanding these symbols and crafting your own sigils, you can tap into the profound energies of the ocean, making your sea magic rituals more potent and transformative.

Chapter 4: Gathering Your Tools

The mysterious allure of the sea has captivated humanity for eons. It's a place where stories of mermaids, sea monsters, and ancient mariners converge, allowing those who are drawn to its depths to experience a type of magic that's both enchanting and powerful. At the heart of this magic, in the practice of sea witchery, lies the importance of ritual tools. These tools, when carefully selected, can enhance your connection to the ocean and amplify the power of your rituals.

Ritual Tools Specific to Sea Witchery

Sea witchery is a unique path within the broader realm of witchcraft. Its tools, inherently tied to the ocean, are brimming with the energy of waves, tides, and marine life. Here are some of the primary tools a sea witch might utilize:

Sea Water: Considered the essence of the ocean, sea water is often used in rituals for purification, blessings, and consecration. It carries with it the energy of the vast ocean, making it an indispensable tool in various spells and rituals.

Shells: Shells, in all their diversity, have been used as symbols of protection, love, and prosperity. Larger shells like the conch can be used as ritual chalices, while smaller ones can serve as containers for ingredients or as representative symbols in spells.

Driftwood: Sculpted by the sea, driftwood is considered a bridge between the terrestrial and marine worlds. It can be used to craft wands, staffs, or even altars.

Sand: Often used to represent the element of Earth in sea witch rituals, sand can be used in jars for spells, as a base for incense burning, or even to draw symbols during rituals.

Seaweed and Sea Plants: These can be dried and used in spells, sachets, or even brewed as magical teas. Their diverse properties, ranging from protection to love attraction, make them invaluable.

Sea Glass: Tumbled and smoothed by the ocean's waves, sea glass is often utilized for protection, healing, and transformation spells.

Sea Stones and Pebbles: Often used as grounding tools, they can also be engraved with sigils or symbols and utilized in spells.

Ethically Collecting Sea Materials

The beauty and power of the sea and its treasures can be tempting for anyone. However, as practitioners of sea witchery, it's vital to remember that the ocean is a living, breathing entity, home to countless creatures and ecosystems. Ethical collection ensures that the balance and sanctity of the ocean remain undisturbed.

Tread Lightly: When you visit the beach or coastal areas, be aware of your surroundings. Ensure you aren't disturbing habitats or wildlife.

Limit Your Collection: While it might be tempting to take home every beautiful shell or piece of driftwood you find, exercise restraint. Only take what you genuinely feel called to and what you'll use.

Avoid Live Specimens: Never take shells with living creatures inside. Not only is this ethically wrong, but using a tool that resulted from harm can also imbue your rituals with negative energies.

Research Protected Areas: Some beaches or coastal regions might be protected due to their ecological significance. Always ensure that you're allowed to collect items from the area.

Leave No Trace: After any ritual or gathering, ensure you leave the area as you found it. Pack away all your belongings and dispose of any waste properly.

Cleansing and Consecrating Your Tools

Once you've ethically sourced your ritual tools, the next step is to cleanse and consecrate them. This process ensures that any lingering energies are removed, and the tools are infused with your intent.

Cleansing:

Sea Water Bath: Submerge your tools in sea water, allowing the essence of the ocean to purify them. If you're unable to access sea water, a mixture of salt and spring water can be an alternative.

Moonlight Bath: Place your tools under the moon, preferably during a full moon, letting the lunar energy cleanse them.

Incense Smoke: Pass your tools through the smoke of sage or other purifying herbs, ensuring they're enveloped and cleansed by the smoke.

Consecrating:

Consecration is the act of dedicating your tools to their sacred purpose. To consecrate:

Hold the tool in your hand and visualize it glowing with a radiant light.

Say a dedication, such as: "With the power of the sea and the moon above, I consecrate this [tool] for my rituals of love, protection, and magic. May it serve its purpose true, in the name of the ocean, vast and blue."

Imagine the tool absorbing this energy and intent.

Your tools are now ready, imbued with the power of the sea and your intentions. Treat them with respect, store them carefully, and they will serve you well in your sea witchcraft journey.

The tools used in sea witchery are not just physical items; they are bridges between you and the vast, mysterious energy of the ocean. Gathering, respecting, and attuning yourself to these tools can deepen your connection with the sea, making your rituals more potent and meaningful. As you tread this path, always remember to harmonize with the rhythms of the ocean, and let its ageless wisdom guide your way.

Chapter 5: The Creatures of the Deep

The ocean is vast, deeper than our imaginations can truly comprehend, and it houses an incredible array of life. Beyond what the human eye perceives, there exists a realm teeming with creatures of lore and legend. The tales of mermaids, selkies, and elusive water spirits have captured human hearts for centuries. These stories, woven intricately with truth and fantasy, inspire us to delve deeper into the mysteries of the sea.

Mermaids: Sirens of the Sea

Mermaids, often referred to as sirens in ancient tales, are among the most renowned creatures of oceanic folklore. With the upper body of a human and the tail of a fish, they are believed to inhabit underwater kingdoms, far removed from the prying eyes of mankind.

The symbolism associated with mermaids is multifaceted. They represent the wild, untamed nature of the sea, embodying both its beauty and its potential for danger. They are guardians of treasures, both materialistic, like gold and jewels, and intangible, like secrets of the deep. In many tales, mermaids possess enchanting voices, capable of luring sailors to their doom or bestowing blessings upon those they deem worthy. They stand as a metaphor for the ocean's seductive, unpredictable nature.

Selkies: Shape-shifters of the Northern Seas

While mermaids have found their place in the folklore of many coastal cultures, selkies are specific to the northern seas, especially in the tales of the Scottish and Irish. Unlike mermaids, selkies are shape-shifters. In the water, they take on the form of seals. But on land, they shed their seal skins and reveal their human forms beneath.

The symbolism of selkies is deeply intertwined with themes of identity, freedom, and duality. The ability to change between seal and human forms represents the struggle between embracing one's true nature and conforming to societal expectations. Many selkie tales focus on themes of captivity and longing, as these beings often find their seal skins stolen, trapping them on land until they can retrieve them.

Water Spirits: The Ethereal Guardians

Water spirits are a more generalized group, encompassing a myriad of beings from different cultures. They can be found in freshwater sources, such as lakes and rivers, as well as in the vast ocean. Nymphs, undines, and naiads are a few examples.

These spirits often serve as guardians of their respective waters. They protect the creatures living within and ensure the natural balance is maintained. Symbolically, water spirits emphasize the significance of purity, flow, and the cyclical nature of life. They remind us of the interconnectedness of all living things and the role water plays in the sustenance of life.

Connecting and Honoring These Beings

To foster a connection with these marine entities, one must approach with respect, understanding, and an open heart. The ocean's lore is vast, and each creature has its own set of rituals, offerings, and chants that resonate most closely with its essence.

For Mermaids: Begin by spending time near the shore, preferably during dawn or dusk, when the veil between worlds is thin. Sing or play enchanting melodies, honoring their reputed musical prowess. Offerings like shells, pearls, or a heartfelt song can draw their attention. Always remember to ask for their guidance or blessings, never demand.

For Selkies: To connect with these beings, one must venture to the colder, rocky shores where seals are commonly found. A token made of driftwood, inscribed with symbols of freedom and the sea, can be a fitting offering. As you stand on the shore, visualize the duality of their existence and send out a silent plea of understanding and respect.

For Water Spirits: Freshwater spirits can be honored by maintaining the cleanliness and sanctity of their homes. Organize or participate in clean-ups of rivers, lakes, or ponds. For oceanic spirits, a small handmade boat with offerings of flowers can be set adrift with a wish or prayer.

In all interactions, the key is genuine reverence. Remember that you're entering their domain and must adhere to the age-old principle: "Take nothing but memories, leave nothing but footprints." Engage in regular meditation, envisioning these entities, and slowly, you'll feel their energies intertwining with yours.

The creatures of the deep are more than just stories; they are symbolic representations of the ocean's many moods and mysteries. By understanding and honoring them, we not only deepen our connection to the sea but also to the profound mysteries and wonders of life itself. The ocean is waiting, and its denizens are eager to share their tales. Dive deep, listen intently, and let your soul be guided by the waves and whispers of the ancient sea.

Chapter 6: Sacred Spaces by the Sea

The sea, with its vast expanse and ever-shifting nature, has long been revered as a powerful and sacred entity. From ancient times to the present, the ocean has been a source of mystery, magic, and spiritual connection for many. In the practice of sea witchery, the shoreline—where the land meets the sea—becomes a liminal space, a threshold between the world of the living and the world of spirits. Creating a sacred space by the sea can be an intimate and transformative experience, opening the door to deeper connections with the ocean and its myriad energies.

Crafting Your Ocean Altar

An ocean altar acts as a focal point for your sea rituals, a space where you can channel the energy of the ocean, honor sea deities, and connect with marine spirits. While the specifics can vary based on personal preferences and traditions, certain elements are commonly found in sea altars.

Materials: Natural items such as seashells, driftwood, seaweed, and sea glass can be used to craft your altar. They act as conduits, drawing in the ocean's energy. Stones like aquamarine, moonstone, and larimar can also be incorporated for their water-affiliated properties.

Placement: If possible, set your altar facing the sea, allowing the altar to be bathed in the ocean's ebb and flow. This isn't always feasible, especially if you're working on a crowded beach, but even a small, discreet altar can be powerful if set with intention.

Centerpiece: Often, practitioners place a centerpiece that holds personal significance—maybe a particularly striking shell, a statue of a sea deity, or a vessel of saltwater drawn from the ocean itself.

Offerings: As with any form of witchcraft, offerings to deities or spirits can be a crucial part of the ritual. Consider things the sea might appreciate: a song, a poem, biodegradable offerings, or even the act of cleaning up the beach around you.

Remember, the most important aspect of your ocean altar is the intention behind it. Whether it's grand and elaborate or simple and discreet, if crafted with respect and genuine connection, it'll serve as a potent tool in your sea witchery.

Finding and Designating Sacred Spaces on the Shore

Not all stretches of the coastline will resonate with you in the same way. The act of finding a sacred space on the shore requires patience, intuition, and a keen sense of awareness.

Listen to the Land: Spend time exploring different parts of the coastline. Sit. Meditate. Listen. Some areas might feel more 'alive' or resonate more deeply with you than others. These are the spaces where the veil between the mundane and the magical feels thinner.

Consider Practicality: While a secluded cove might feel enchanting, if it's a two-hour trek to get there, you might not visit it as often. Balance spiritual resonance with practicality.

Claiming a Space: Once you've found your spot, spend time there. Get to know its rhythms and moods. Over time, as you perform rituals and engage in meditation in this space, it'll become imbued with your energy, making it even more sacred and potent.

Respect and Stewardship: Always remember that while this space might be sacred to you, it's part of a larger ecosystem. Take care not to harm or disrupt local wildlife. Consider adopting a practice of cleaning up the beach or making other positive environmental impacts as part of your stewardship.

Protective Measures for Working by the Sea

The sea is beautiful and powerful, but it can also be unpredictable and sometimes dangerous. When working magic by its shores, it's essential to prioritize safety.

Natural Dangers: Be aware of tides. An incoming tide can quickly cut off access to parts of the beach, leaving you stranded. Always check tide schedules before heading out. Likewise, be wary of wildlife—some creatures, like jellyfish or certain types of seaweed, can be harmful.

Spiritual Protections: Just as the sea is home to benevolent spirits, there might also be entities less kindly disposed. Before starting any ritual, cast a protective circle or employ other protective measures familiar to you. This creates a boundary between you and any potential negative influences.

Respect the Sea's Power: No matter how experienced or confident you are, never underestimate the ocean's power. Avoid turning your back on the waves, especially during stormy conditions or when the sea is particularly rough.

Leave No Trace: As part of your protective measures, ensure that you leave the beach as you found it—or even better. Any candles, offerings, or other ritual components should be removed or properly disposed of, ensuring that the sacred space remains pristine for others and for future visits.

Creating a sacred space by the sea is a deeply personal and transformative act. It allows for a direct communion with one of nature's most potent forces. With respect, awareness, and intention, this practice can become a cornerstone of your journey as a sea witch, leading to profound insights and powerful magic. Always remember that the sea gives generously, but it also demands respect. Approach it with an open heart and a keen awareness, and the depths of its mysteries will unfold before you.

Chapter 7: Rituals for Ebb Tides

The rhythmic dance of the ocean, with its perpetual ebb and flow, is a testament to the universe's ever-changing nature. The sea teaches us that every high has a low, and after every surge, there is a retreat. The ebb tide, or the receding tide, stands as a symbol of release, letting go, and a return to calm. It's during this time that the ocean, in its silent wisdom, provides the perfect atmosphere for rituals that pertain to banishing, shedding, and purification.

Rituals for Releasing, Banishing, and Letting Go

The Sea Salt Release Ritual

Ingredients:

Sea salt (collected or purchased)

A small bowl of water (preferably ocean water)

A piece of paper and pen

A fire-safe container

Steps:

Stand or sit by the shoreline, tuning into the sound and rhythm of the receding waves.

On the paper, write down what you wish to release or let go—this could be a habit, a person, a memory, or even a feeling.

Mix a pinch of sea salt into the bowl of water while focusing on your intention of purification.

Dip the paper into the salted water, allowing it to get thoroughly soaked. As you do this, visualize the water cleansing and absorbing the energy of what you're letting go.

Safely light the wet paper in the fire-safe container. Watch it burn, imagining the flames transforming the energy, and the smoke carrying away your burdens to the universe.

Dispose of the ashes into the sea, thanking the ocean for its cleansing power.

The Seashell Banishing Spell

Seashells are natural gifts from the ocean, each unique in its pattern and energy. This ritual uses the shell as a vessel to absorb and banish negative influences.

Ingredients:

A seashell (preferably one you've found)

Black salt (a mixture of sea salt and charcoal)

Anointing oil (like sage or cedarwood)

Steps:

Hold the seashell in your hand, feeling its texture and tuning into its energy.

Anoint the shell with a few drops of oil, stating your intention of banishment.

Fill the shell with black salt.

Whisper to the shell what you wish to banish. Visualize this negativity being trapped within the salt.

Bury the shell in the sand or at the beach, allowing the earth to neutralize and transform the trapped energies.

The Importance of the Receding Tide

Tides are the result of the gravitational pull of the moon and, to a lesser extent, the sun. The receding tide, in particular, holds significance in sea witchery because of its symbolic and energetic implications.

Just as the water pulls away from the shore, so can we use this time to symbolically pull away from things that no longer serve us. It's a period where the sea demonstrates the art of detachment, showing that sometimes withdrawing and letting go is necessary for rejuvenation and new beginnings.

The ebb tide is also crucial for revealing treasures that were previously submerged or hidden. In the same vein, when we shed and release, we often uncover hidden strengths, talents, or facets of our souls that remained unnoticed or suppressed.

Sea Spells for Clearing Negative Energy

Ocean Breath Clearing Meditation

The simplest yet most profound way to connect with the sea's energy is through meditative breathing.

Steps:

Sit comfortably by the shoreline, close your eyes and tune into your breath.

With every inhale, visualize the ocean's vast energy filling you with clarity and peace.

With every exhale, imagine releasing any negativity, stress, or tension into the waves, letting the sea carry it away.

Continue for at least 10 minutes or until you feel a distinct sense of lightness and purification.

Wave Wash Spell

Ingredients:

A piece of cloth (representative of what you want to cleanse – it can be an article of clothing, a symbolic handkerchief, etc.)

A natural biodegradable soap or essential oil

Steps:

As the tide begins to ebb, approach the water's edge.

Wet the cloth in the sea, lathering it with the soap or just a few drops of essential oil.

As you wash the cloth in the waves, focus on the intention of the ocean waves clearing away all negative energies.

Once cleansed, wring out the cloth and leave it to dry under the moonlight.

Driftwood Barrier Ritual

Driftwood, having traveled great distances and transformed by the sea's energy, can serve as a powerful protective talisman against negativity.

Ingredients:

A piece of driftwood

A protective stone like black tourmaline or obsidian

Steps:

Hold both the driftwood and stone in your hands, charging them with your intention of protection.

Bury the stone in the sand, marking the spot.

Place the driftwood pointing away from the marked spot towards the sea, symbolizing a barrier that directs negative energies away from you and into the ocean for cleansing.

Leave the arrangement overnight, and retrieve the stone the next day, keeping it with you as a protective amulet.

The ebb tide is not merely a retreat of the sea but a powerful phase that offers a serene backdrop for rituals of release. The sea, in its vastness, reminds us that we, too, are boundless in our ability to rejuvenate, renew, and reinvent ourselves. As the waves recede, they take with them the old, making space for the new, and in this sacred dance of give and take, we find the profound lessons of detachment and rebirth.

Chapter 8: Rituals for Flow Tides

The dance of the tides, perpetually synchronized with the celestial ballet of the moon and sun, forms a vital cornerstone of sea witchery. As the waves retreat during the ebb, they take with them that which is no longer needed, cleansing and purifying. But when the tide flows, it brings forth new energies, vibrant potential, and the nourishing essence of the deep blue.

Flow tides, or rising tides, represent periods of growth, expansion, and abundance. It's during these times that the sea shares with us its secrets for attracting blessings, manifesting desires, and accumulating abundance in various aspects of our lives. This chapter will delve deep into rituals, spells, and practices tailored to harness the formidable force of the flow tides.

Ritual of the Rising Tide: Attracting Abundant Blessings

Materials:

A bowl of fresh seawater

Silver coin or charm

White or blue candle

Fragrance of jasmine or rosemary oil

Procedure:

Find a quiet spot on the shore during the onset of a rising tide.

Sit comfortably, placing your tools in front of you. Begin by lighting the candle.

Dip the silver coin or charm into the bowl of seawater, visualizing it absorbing the sea's magnetic energy.

While holding the charm above the bowl, recite:

"By the power of the rising tide, by the sea's vast expanse so wide,

I call forth abundance, far and wide, let prosperity by my side reside."

Anoint yourself with the jasmine or rosemary oil, sealing in the energies of attraction.

Extinguish the candle, bury the coin or charm in the sand, and let the sea claim it as the tide rises. This serves as an offering and a symbol of your trust in the ocean's generosity.

Moonlit Manifestation Spell

The moon, being a vital influence on the tides, can amplify the energy of your sea spells when combined with the power of the flow tide.

Materials:

Moonstone or aquamarine gem

A parchment or piece of paper

A small bottle with a cork

A strand of your hair or a personal trinket

Procedure:

Under the moonlight, preferably during a waxing or full moon phase, write your heart's desire on the parchment.

Fold the parchment and place it inside the bottle, along with the moonstone or aquamarine gem and your personal item.

Seal the bottle with the cork and whisper to it your intention. Hold it close to your heart, and then release it into the rising tide.

As the bottle drifts with the flow tide, visualize your desires manifesting and becoming part of your reality.

Sea Spell for Love, Luck, and Prosperity

While the sea holds immense power for abundance and manifestation, it also cradles energies of love and luck within its depths.

Materials:

Three sea shells (preferably found during a rising tide)

A strand of seaweed or a piece of driftwood

A pink, green, and gold ribbon

Procedure:

At the shore, place the three shells in front of you.

Assign each shell a purpose: one for love, another for luck, and the last for prosperity.

Taking the strand of seaweed or driftwood, connect the shells, envisioning them being linked by the energy of your intentions.

As you bind them, chant:

"Gifts from the sea, shells three,

Bring love, luck, and prosperity to me."

Tie each shell with one of the ribbons: pink for love, green for luck, and gold for prosperity.

Bury the connected shells at the water's edge, letting the rising tide wash over them, sealing in your intentions.

The ebb and flow of the tides serve as a poignant reminder of the cycles of life. Just as the sea can recede, taking away the old, it can also surge forth, full of promise and new beginnings. Harnessing the energies of the flow tide is about understanding this potent dynamic, tapping into a force of nature that's as old as time.

As you carry out these rituals, remember to do so with a heart full of gratitude and reverence for the sea and its mysteries. The ocean, in its vastness and depth, mirrors the boundless possibilities within each one of us. And as you stand at the shoreline, with the rising tide lapping at your feet, know that you are intertwined with this ancient, powerful magic—a dance of attraction, manifestation, and bountiful abundance.

Chapter 9: Sea Meditation and Astral Voyages

Meditation has long been celebrated as a gateway to inner peace, heightened awareness, and spiritual connection. The vastness of the ocean, with its rhythmic waves and infinite horizon, naturally beckons the meditative mind. Beyond this physical realm lies the astral, where visions transform into experiential journeys and the boundaries of reality blend with the fantastical.

Techniques for Meditating by the Sea

Finding a meditative state by the sea is a unique experience, distinct from any other natural setting. The ebb and flow of the tides, the song of the waves, and the scent of salt in the air coalesce to create a backdrop that lulls the mind into deep introspection.

Choosing the Right Spot: Begin by selecting a location. Whether it's a sandy shore, a rocky outcrop, or a secluded cove, it's essential to find a space where you feel safe and undisturbed. Sit or lie down, ensuring you're comfortable, and orient yourself to face the ocean. Close your eyes and take a few deep breaths, allowing the salty breeze to fill your lungs and expel any tension.

The Breath of the Ocean: Align your breathing with the rhythm of the waves. Inhale as the wave approaches and exhale as it recedes. This synchronization not only grounds you in the present moment but also forges a profound connection between your inner self and the vast expanse of the sea.

Sound Immersion: Instead of trying to block out external noises, embrace the symphony of the sea. The cries of seagulls, the gentle rustling of seaweed, and the distant echo of crashing waves can enhance your meditative experience, acting as natural mantras that guide your thoughts deeper into tranquility.

Oceanic Guided Visualizations

Visualization is a powerful tool in meditation. When combined with the already potent energies of the sea, it can offer transformative experiences. Here's a guided oceanic visualization to immerse you in the depths of the ocean:

Begin with your regular meditation routine, deepening your breath and releasing tension from your body. As your eyelids grow heavy, imagine a shimmering orb of blue light hovering above the water's surface. This orb represents the essence of the ocean, a beacon guiding you on your journey.

Now, visualize yourself floating gently above the waves, drawn towards this luminous sphere. As you approach, the orb expands, enveloping you in its glow. Feel its energy seeping into your pores, infusing you with the mysteries of the deep.

Gradually, the light starts to descend, pulling you beneath the surface. Below, a world of wonder awaits: vibrant coral reefs teeming with life, ancient shipwrecks holding tales of old, and deep trenches echoing the heartbeat of the ocean. Swim with playful dolphins, glide alongside majestic whales, and feel the weightlessness of this underwater realm.

When you're ready to return, visualize the blue orb gently floating you back to the surface. As you emerge, carry the tranquility and insights from the oceanic depths with you.

Astral Travel to Underwater Realms

The astral plane is an ethereal realm where the soul travels free from the physical body. The sea, being a space of vast energy and deep mystery, hosts several astral realms. Venturing into these underwater astral domains can be an enlightening experience, offering insights into ancient wisdom and connecting you with marine entities.

Preparing for the Journey: Before attempting astral travel, it's essential to be well-versed in grounding and protection techniques. Ensure you're in a calm state of mind, free from distractions. Surround yourself with protective symbols, perhaps seashells or sand, to keep a connection with the ocean.

The Descent: Start by visualizing the ocean as a vast, infinite space below you. Imagine your astral self diving into this expanse, moving deeper and deeper. As you descend, you might feel a change in pressure, a shift in temperature, or even hear different sounds – these are all indications of your entry into the astral sea realms.

Exploring the Astral Seas: Here, the water isn't a barrier but a medium. Breathe it in, let it nourish you. In this astral ocean, cities of light may emerge from the depths, merfolk might extend invitations to their domains, and portals to other realities could appear. Engage with these visions, but always with respect and caution.

Returning to the Physical: Once your exploration concludes, visualize yourself ascending towards the surface. Feel the boundaries of the astral and physical merging as you realign with your physical form. Ground yourself, perhaps by holding onto a piece of sea glass or rock, and take a moment to process the journey you undertook.

The sea, in its vastness, holds realms both real and ethereal. Through sea meditation and astral voyages, we can tap into these mysteries, drawing insights, peace, and a deeper connection to the universe's rhythms. Whether you're on a sandy shore or deep in the astral oceans, the sea's embrace is a testament to the endless possibilities that lie in the depths of our consciousness.

Chapter 10: Potions and Elixirs from the Ocean's Bounty

The ocean, vast and infinite, holds a treasure trove of magical ingredients within its depths. From the briny kiss of its waters to the swaying dance of seaweeds, every drop and fragment embodies the boundless energy of the sea. Potions and elixirs brewed with the ocean's bounty carry the transformative power of the tides, capable of healing, empowering, and guiding those who partake of them.

Brewing Magical Seawater

Seawater is the very essence of the ocean. It is a complex solution of minerals, salts, and organic matter, each contributing its unique energy to the magical blend. Collecting seawater for magical purposes requires intention, respect, and an understanding of the ebb and flow of the tides.

Collection:

Choose a time when the tides are turning, either from low to high or high to low. This is a moment of powerful transition, and the water collected at these times is particularly potent. As you gather the water, envision your purpose, be it healing, protection, or transformation. Whisper your intent into the waves, thanking the ocean for its gift.

Purification:

While seawater is already a potent mixture, it's essential to purify it before use. This can be done by filtering the water to remove any large debris and then boiling it. As you heat the water, visualize any impurities, both physical and energetic, being lifted away by the steam. Once cooled, store your magical seawater in a glass container, ready for use.

Crafting Elixirs Using Seaweed, Salt, and Other Oceanic Ingredients

The ocean offers a myriad of ingredients, each with unique properties and energies.

Seaweed Elixir:

Seaweed, with its deep connection to the ocean floor and rich mineral content, is ideal for grounding and nourishing elixirs.

Ingredients:

A handful of fresh seaweed (like kelp or nori)

Magical seawater

A pinch of sea salt

Procedure:

Cleanse the seaweed, ensuring all sand and foreign particles are removed.

In a pot, combine the seaweed and magical seawater.

Allow the mixture to simmer gently for about 20 minutes.

Strain the mixture, add a pinch of sea salt, and transfer to a glass bottle. Your seaweed elixir is now ready. Consume it to connect deeply with the ocean's grounding energies.

Salt Elixir:

Sea salt, a product of evaporated seawater, retains the ocean's potent energy. This elixir is excellent for purification and protection.

Ingredients:

Coarse sea salt

Spring water or purified water

Procedure:

In a glass container, mix a tablespoon of sea salt with spring water.

Seal the container and let it sit under moonlight for one full lunar cycle.

After this period, strain the solution, storing the salt-infused water. This elixir can be used in rituals, baths, or even consumed in tiny amounts to purify one's energy.

Other Oceanic Ingredients:

Apart from seaweed and salt, other oceanic ingredients like sea moss, sea lavender, and even pearls can be infused in elixirs. Each ingredient offers distinct properties—sea moss for abundance, sea lavender for peace, and pearls for purity.

Benefits and Cautionary Advice About Ingesting Sea-Based Potions

Ingesting the ocean's essence, whether through elixirs or potions, can be deeply transformative. These concoctions can align one's energy with the vastness of the sea, bringing clarity, balance, and a deeper connection to nature.

Benefits:

Connection to the Ocean: Consuming sea-based potions enhances one's bond with the ocean, making rituals more potent.

Physical Nourishment: Many oceanic ingredients, especially seaweed, are rich in minerals and nutrients that can nourish the body.

Energetic Balance: The rhythmic ebb and flow of the ocean can mirror our energies, helping bring balance and calm.

Cautionary Advice:

Always Purify: Whether it's seawater, seaweed, or any other oceanic ingredient, always ensure they are cleaned and purified before consumption.

Know the Source: Ensure that all ingredients are ethically sourced and free from pollutants.

Mindful Consumption: Begin with small quantities to gauge your body's reaction. Not all elixirs or potions are meant for consumption; some are for external use only.

Consult Professionals: Before ingesting any potion or elixir, especially if consumed regularly, consult with a healthcare professional to ensure it's safe, particularly if you have health conditions or are on medications.

In the dance of waves and whispers of the shore, the ocean shares its secrets with those willing to listen. With care, respect, and a deep understanding of its bounty, one can harness the sea's magic in potions and elixirs, creating blends that heal, empower, and transform. As with all magical practices, intention is key. Let every drop you brew or sip be a testament to your bond with the vast, wondrous world of the sea.

Chapter 11: Crafting Sea Talismans and Amulets

The ocean is not just a vast expanse of saltwater; it is a treasure trove of powerful magical items waiting to be discovered. From the delicate whispers of seashells to the silent strength of driftwood, each item carries with it a unique energy, influenced by the tides, the moon, and the creatures that call the ocean home. In this chapter, we will dive deep into the craft of creating sea talismans and amulets, tangible manifestations of oceanic magic.

Creating Protective Charms Using Shells, Sea Glass, and Driftwood

Every wave that crashes onto the shore brings with it gifts. Among these are shells, sea glass, and driftwood, each holding the power to protect, guide, and heal.

Shells: Each shell, with its unique shape and pattern, holds a story. Some may have housed a creature, while others may have been homes to tiny organisms. To create a protective talisman using shells, first, find one that resonates with you. Hold it in your hand and listen; sometimes, you'll hear more than just the echo of the ocean. Once chosen, cleanse the shell in saltwater, allowing it to absorb the sea's purifying energies. You can then inscribe symbols or sigils onto the shell using a sharp tool. These symbols can represent protection, guidance, or any intention you wish to imbue into your talisman.

Sea Glass: These are fragments of glass bottles or objects that have been smoothed and frosted over time by the action of waves and sand. Their journey from sharp shards to smooth pieces symbolizes transformation and resilience. Choose a piece of sea glass that calls out to you, preferably one with a color that matches your protective intentions. Blue, for instance, resonates with calm and tranquility, while green is often associated with healing. Once chosen, wrap the sea glass with silver or copper wire, turning it into a pendant. As you do so, focus on your intention, weaving it into your creation.

Driftwood: This wood has been shaped by its time in the ocean, representing endurance and adaptability. To create a protective amulet with driftwood, select a piece that feels right in your hand—neither too big nor too small. Using natural twine or string, you can attach other protective elements like small shells or stones. As you tie each knot, focus on the protective energies of the ocean, visualizing a barrier forming around you.

The Magic of Pearls and Coral

Pearls: These luminous gems from the deep are born from irritation. When an oyster senses an irritant, like a grain of sand, it secretes layers of nacre around it, resulting in the creation of a pearl. This process symbolizes the transformation of adversity into beauty. Pearls are known to attract wealth, luck, and offer protection. They also amplify the wearer's integrity, loyalty, and purity. To use pearls in talisman-making, you can incorporate them into jewelry designs or even sew them onto cloth pouches filled with other protective herbs and stones.

Coral: This organic material is formed by colonies of tiny marine animals. It symbolizes life, blood force energy, and the vast web of interconnectedness. Red coral, in particular, is known for its protective qualities, especially against negative energies. For crafting, choose a piece of coral that has been ethically sourced. Wear it as a pendant or carry a small piece with you in a pouch to serve as a protective charm.

Charging and Activating Your Sea Talismans

No matter how beautiful or intricate your talisman or amulet might be, it remains a decorative object until it's charged and activated with intent. Here's a simple ritual to harness the ocean's energy:

Cleansing: Begin by cleansing your talisman. This can be done by placing it in a bowl of saltwater under the moonlight or burying it in the sand at the beach, allowing the natural energies to purify it.

Charging: During a time when you feel most connected to the ocean—perhaps at high tide or during a full moon—hold your talisman in your hands and close your eyes. Visualize the ocean's waves enveloping it, filling it with energy. Feel the ebb and flow of the tides and the pull of the moon. As you do this, whisper your intentions into the talisman.

Activation: Once charged, it's time to activate your talisman. Wear it against your skin or keep it close to you for seven days and seven nights, allowing its energies to synchronize with yours.

Maintenance: Over time, the energies of your talisman may wane. Recharge and reactivate it by repeating the process or by simply spending time with it by the ocean, soaking in the sea's rejuvenating energies.

In the end, the power of your sea talisman or amulet is derived not just from the materials it's made from, but from the intentions and energies you infuse into it. Wear it with pride, knowing you carry a piece of the ocean's magic with you, guarding and guiding you through life's ebbs and flows.

Chapter 12: Celebrating Ocean Sabbats

Sea-Based Celebrations for the Wheel of the Year

The Wheel of the Year is a cyclical calendar used by many neopagan traditions, marking the changing of seasons and the ebb and flow of life. For the sea witch, these changes are not just experienced on land but are mirrored in the tides, the migration of marine life, and the temperaments of the ocean itself. By adapting the traditional sabbats to sea-based celebrations, one can tap into the profound connection between the rhythm of the earth and the pulse of the ocean.

Imbolc - Awakening the Sea

As the world slowly emerges from winter, the ocean too begins to stir with life. Imbolc, usually celebrated on February 1st or 2nd, signifies the first hint of spring. During this time, the sea witch can focus on invoking the rejuvenating energies of the ocean.

Ritual: Stand at the shore during low tide and light a white or blue candle. As the tide begins to come in, visualize the ocean's energy growing, just as the light increases each day. Whisper your intentions and wishes for the coming months into a seashell and place it gently into the waves.

Ostara - Balance of Land and Sea

Falling on the Spring Equinox, Ostara represents balance. Day and night are of equal length. For sea witches, this is a time to honor the equilibrium between land and sea.

Ritual: Collect equal amounts of sea water and fresh spring water. Mix them in a ceremonial bowl, stirring with a wand made of driftwood. Meditate on balancing your own energies, the give and take, and the importance of harmony in all things.

Beltane - Dance of the Dolphins

Beltane, celebrated on May 1st, heralds the height of spring's fertility. The ocean too bursts forth in vibrant life. Dolphins, often seen frolicking during this time, can be symbols for Beltane's playful and passionate energy.

Ritual: Craft a simple dolphin amulet from clay or carry a representation of a dolphin. Head to the beach and dance along the shoreline, embracing the joyous energies of Beltane and the playfulness of the dolphins.

Litha - Embracing the Ocean's Warmth

Midsummer, or Litha, falls on the Summer Solstice, the longest day of the year. It's a time to celebrate the sun at its peak and the warmth of the ocean.

Ritual: Create a sun circle on the beach using stones, seaweed, or shells. In its center, place a bowl of sea water. As the sun sets, reflect on its warmth and energy. Dip your fingers into the bowl, feeling the warmth of the sun-charged sea water, and anoint your forehead, heart, and wrists.

Lammas - Harvest of the Sea

Lammas, or Lughnasadh, celebrated on August 1st, marks the beginning of the harvest season. The sea offers its own bounties: seaweeds are lush and seafood is abundant.

Ritual: Prepare a feast using the bounties of the sea. Give thanks to the ocean and the deities of the sea. Consider leaving a small offering, such as biodegradable flowers, at the shore as a token of gratitude.

Mabon - The Ocean's Ebb and Flow

The Autumn Equinox, Mabon, is a time of reflection and balance. Just as day and night stand equal, the sea reflects the balance of ebb and flow.

Ritual: On a beach or rocky shoreline, create two altars: one for the ebb and one for the flow. On the ebb altar, place items that represent things you wish to release or diminish. On the flow altar, place symbols of what you wish to attract. Meditate between them, feeling the balance and rhythm of the ocean and your life.

Samhain - Ancestors of the Deep

Marking the end of the harvest season and the start of winter, Samhain is a time to honor the ancestors and the spiritual world. The sea, with its depths and mysteries, holds its own ancestors.

Ritual: Create a water lantern using biodegradable materials. On it, write messages or names of ancestors, including ancient sea beings or deities. At twilight, release the lantern onto gentle waters, watching as it carries your reverence and love into the embrace of the ocean.

Yule - The Ocean's Slumber

On the Winter Solstice, the shortest day of the year, Yule celebrates the rebirth of the sun. The sea, though still mighty, takes on a semblance of slumber in many parts of the world.

Ritual: Gather around a bonfire on the beach. Share tales of sea deities, mermaids, and ancient ocean legends. As the fire burns, throw in dried seaweed as an offering, symbolizing the warmth and light returning to both the land and the sea.

Honoring Sea Deities During Sabbats

Each sabbat provides an opportunity to honor specific sea deities. For instance, Poseidon, the god of the sea in Greek mythology, could be honored during Litha for his fiery temperament. Yemaya, the Yoruban goddess of the ocean, could be revered during Mabon for her maternal and protective qualities. Understanding and building relationships with these deities can deepen the sabbat experience.

Special Rituals and Feasts for Each Sabbat

The ocean provides an abundance of materials and energies for special rituals. Seaweed can be used for protection spells during Samhain. Sand dollars, often associated with divine energy due to their star-like design, can be incorporated into Yule celebrations symbolizing the returning sun.

Feasts, integral to many sabbats, can focus on the bounties of the ocean. Fresh seafood, seaweed salads, and salted treats can grace the table, offering a taste of the sea's generosity.

Incorporating the ocean into sabbat celebrations not only aligns a sea witch with the rhythms of the earth but also with the ever-changing, yet constant, rhythms of the mighty ocean. The waves that crash upon the shore with the turning of the Wheel of the Year remind us of the interconnectedness of all things and the sacred dance of land and sea.

Chapter 13: Navigating Storms: Rituals for Turbulent Times

The sea, in all its vastness and beauty, is not always calm. There are moments when it rages with tempestuous energy, mirroring the storms we encounter in our own lives. The waves crash harder, the winds blow with fierce intensity, and the atmosphere becomes charged with a raw, untamed power. Just as we experience emotional and situational tempests, so does the ocean display its wilder side.

Harnessing the energy of these sea storms can be a potent tool in navigating our own personal challenges. They offer us lessons in resilience, strength, and the inevitable ebb and flow of life. This chapter delves deep into the heart of these sea storms, offering rituals for protection, grounding, and transformation during life's turbulent times.

Harnessing the Energy of Sea Storms

Sea storms, while often seen as destructive, carry with them a powerful force that can be harnessed for transformative magic. When the ocean is in uproar, it releases an energy that is both chaotic and cleansing. This energy can be captured and channeled to break through stagnation, clear out negativity, and initiate change.

To harness this energy, one must first learn to respect it. Stand at the edge of the sea during a storm, safely distanced from the crashing waves. Feel the wind on your face, hear the roar of the waves, and taste the salt in the air. With every gust and wave crash, visualize the storm's energy merging with your own, charging you with its raw power.

You can also collect storm water in a jar or bottle. This water, charged with the storm's essence, can be used in rituals, spells, and as a base for potions intended to evoke change, power, and cleansing.

Rituals for Protection

In the face of life's tempests, protection becomes paramount. The sea, with its vastness, can serve as a guardian force.

Sea Salt Circle: Create a circle using sea salt around your sacred space or around yourself. As you lay down the salt, envision it forming a barrier, repelling negativity and harm. Chant, "By the sea's might and storm's power, I am shielded every hour."

Stormy Talisman: Find a stone or shell during a sea storm. Hold it close and say, "By the storm and sea's rage, protect me, be my cage." Carry this with you or place it in your home as a protective amulet.

Rituals for Grounding

During turbulent times, grounding is essential. It allows us to remain balanced, even when surrounded by chaos.

Ocean Breath Meditation: Stand or sit by the stormy sea. Breathe in sync with the waves. Inhale as the waves retreat, exhale as they crash. This mirrors the natural rhythm of life and grounds your energy.

Sandy Footing: Walk barefoot on wet sand during a storm. Visualize roots extending from your feet into the earth, anchoring you. As you walk, recite, "With every step in stormy times, I'm grounded, I'm aligned."

Rituals for Transformation

Sea storms symbolize change and transformation. Their powerful energies can be harnessed to instigate personal growth and metamorphosis.

Wave Release Ritual: Write down aspects of your life you wish to transform or release on biodegradable paper. Stand at the water's edge and read them out loud to the stormy sea. Then, release the paper into the waves, visualizing the sea taking away your burdens and replacing them with its strength.

Storm Dance: Dance on the beach during a storm. Let the winds guide your movements. As you dance, envision yourself shedding old patterns and embracing the change the storm brings.

Connecting with the Tempestuous Side of the Ocean

To truly harness the power of sea storms, one must establish a deep connection with the ocean's tempestuous side. This means understanding that the ocean, like us, has moments of calm and moments of chaos.

Spend time by the ocean during different weather patterns. Meditate on its changing moods. Journal your experiences, noting any insights or revelations that arise. Over time, you'll begin to see the parallels between the ocean's tempests and your own, and you'll learn to navigate both with grace, resilience, and a deep sense of connection.

Sea storms, with their raw power, mirror the challenges we face in life. By respecting this power, harnessing it, and connecting deeply with the ocean's wild side, we can navigate our own storms with a renewed sense of purpose, protection, and transformation. Let the ocean's tempests guide you, protect you, and ultimately, transform you.

Chapter 14: Ethical Considerations and Environmental Awareness

At the very core of sea witchcraft lies a profound connection to the oceans, an immense force that has played a pivotal role in shaping life on Earth. This bond is not just spiritual, but also ecological, and as practitioners of the craft, we have a responsibility to ensure our practices don't harm the very essence we draw power from.

Practicing Sea Witchcraft with Respect for Marine Life

For many sea witches, the allure of the deep blue is intertwined with the magnificent creatures that reside within its depths. From the microscopic plankton to the grand whales, every being plays a vital role in the marine ecosystem. When we engage in rituals, whether collecting materials or performing rites at the shore, it's paramount to prioritize the well-being of these creatures.

Firstly, when collecting items such as shells, it's essential to ensure that they are unoccupied. Taking a shell that is a home to a creature not only disrupts its life but can also weaken the spiritual potency of your ritual. Dead shells, those cast away by their previous inhabitants, carry the pure energies of the sea, untainted by the trauma of displacement.

Similarly, while seaweeds are potent in rituals, one should gather them sparingly and never uproot them entirely. Seaweeds anchor the ocean floor and provide food and shelter for many marine creatures. It's best to take only what floats free or to snip a small part, allowing the plant to continue thriving.

The respect we show to marine life is a reflection of our respect for the craft. If the oceans and their inhabitants suffer, the very core of sea witchcraft weakens. Therefore, always practice with awareness and make choices that promote the well-being of marine life.

Advocacy for Ocean Conservation

Sea witchcraft isn't just a personal journey; it's a collective responsibility. Our oceans are facing unprecedented challenges, from pollution and overfishing to climate change impacts like coral bleaching. Advocating for the conservation of the oceans is not just an act of altruism; it's a necessary part of being a sea witch.

Many ancient spells and rituals involve the release of items into the sea. However, in modern times, with the knowledge of how pollutants can affect marine ecosystems, it's crucial to adapt these practices. Biodegradable offerings or symbolic releases, where an item is spiritually "released" but physically kept or disposed of properly, can be just as potent.

Engaging in beach clean-ups, supporting marine conservation initiatives, and even educating others about the importance of the oceans can amplify the impact of your sea magic. When you heal the ocean, even through non-magical means, you strengthen your bond and enhance your craft.

The Interconnectedness of Sea Magic and Environmentalism

Sea magic is deeply rooted in the rhythms and flows of the ocean. The energy we tap into, the spirits we communicate with, and the rituals we perform are all reflections of the state of the ocean. Environmentalism and sea witchcraft are intrinsically linked; one cannot thrive without the other.

Consider the power of water in your rituals. The purity and vibrancy of that water determine its effectiveness. Polluted waters, burdened with toxins and devoid of life, can hinder the potency of your spells. As the health of our oceans declines, so does the effectiveness of our sea magic.

Beyond the immediate, there's a broader, more profound connection to ponder. The ocean is a mirror, reflecting the collective consciousness of the world. When we harm the ocean, either through negligence or direct action, we are, in essence, casting a dark spell upon ourselves. It's a ripple effect: what we send out, comes back.

Incorporate environmentalism into your daily practices. Make sustainable choices, reduce your carbon footprint, and stand against practices that harm marine ecosystems. When you defend the ocean, you're not just being an environmentalist; you're being a true sea witch. The spells you cast, the energy you harness, and the rituals you perform will be imbued with a power that only comes from a genuine, heartfelt connection to the ocean.

The path of the sea witch is not just one of individual spiritual growth but is a journey intertwined with the very pulse of our planet's oceans. To truly harness the power of the sea is to understand its fragility and to advocate for its protection. Our craft and the well-being of the oceans are deeply interconnected, and as practitioners of sea magic, we bear the sacred responsibility of ensuring this bond remains unbroken.

Chapter 15: Nurturing Your Connection with the Sea

The rhythm of the waves, the salty breeze, and the seemingly infinite horizon—these are not just components of the sea but sentiments that stay with us long after we've left its shores. Yet, for those who have been profoundly touched by the ocean, there exists a desire to maintain that connection daily, even when miles away from the coast. This chapter explores practices to keep that connection alive and thriving, every day.

Daily Practices to Stay Connected to the Ocean, Even When Far From It

Being away from the coast doesn't mean you can't resonate with the energy of the ocean. Here are ways to imbue your day with oceanic mindfulness:

Morning Meditations with Ocean Sounds: Begin your day by immersing yourself in the sound of waves. Countless apps and online platforms offer ocean soundtracks. Listen, breathe deeply, and visualize yourself standing on the shore, feeling the waves tickle your feet.

Salt Baths: As you draw a bath, add sea salts, ensuring you immerse in the ocean's healing minerals. As you soak, close your eyes and envision the expansive sea, its depth and mysteries waiting to be discovered.

Wear Ocean-Inspired Jewelry: Adorning yourself with pieces made of shells, sea glass, or oceanic stones like aquamarine and larimar can be a daily reminder of your bond with the sea.

Ocean Scented Incense and Oils: Fill your living space with the fragrance of the ocean. Whether it's seaweed-based scents, a fresh marine fragrance, or the sweet smell reminiscent of tropical beaches, these aromas can instantly transport your senses.

Keeping a Sea Journal

Maintaining a sea journal can serve as a therapeutic practice, allowing you to document your feelings, experiences, and observations related to the ocean. Here's how you can embark on this written journey:

Document Your Seaside Experiences: Every time you visit the sea, write down your feelings, the sights you saw, the creatures you observed, and even the conversations you had. Over time, this will become a beautiful memoir of your sea adventures.

Sketch and Paint: Let your sea journal be a canvas. Draw the waves, the setting sun, or the spiral of a unique shell you found. If words can't express it, colors might.

Paste Keepsakes: Found a particularly beautiful piece of driftwood or a dried seaweed fragment? Add these to your journal. It becomes a tactile memory, something you can touch and feel, instantly taking you back to that moment by the sea.

Moon and Tide Observations: As you grow in your sea witch practice, observing and documenting the moon phases and tides can be crucial. Note down your feelings during different tides and moon phases, and over time, you may see patterns revealing the ocean's subtle influence on your emotions.

Building a Personal Relationship with the Sea and its Spirits

The sea is alive, not just with marine life but with spirits, myths, and energies that have been revered for centuries. To truly nurture your bond with the ocean, it's essential to foster a relationship with these entities:

Honor the Spirits: From mermaids to water nymphs and ancient sea deities like Poseidon and Amphitrite, acknowledging these spirits in your rituals and daily life can intensify your connection. Light a blue candle in their honor or simply send out a prayer of gratitude to them.

Beach Cleanups: One of the most profound ways to honor the sea and its spirits is by ensuring its cleanliness and health. Participate in or organize beach cleanups. Every piece of trash you remove is a step closer to a cleaner ocean and a stronger bond with its spirits.

Talk to the Sea: It might sound whimsical, but conversing with the ocean can be a transformative experience. Stand at the shore, let your feelings flow, speak of your dreams, fears, hopes, and listen. The waves might not reply in words, but the rhythmic ebb and flow can often bring clarity and answers.

Offerings: Give back to the sea. Offerings could be as simple as a song, a dance, or even a silent promise to protect its vast expanse. However, always ensure that your offerings are biodegradable and won't harm marine life.

In essence, nurturing your connection with the sea is a journey of the heart and spirit. It's about remembering the pull of the tides even when you're miles away, about penning down memories that can transport you back to the shore, and about honoring the age-old spirits that have been guardians of the oceanic realms. As you integrate these practices, the sea doesn't remain just a place you visit; it becomes a part of you, its whispers guiding you, its depths inspiring you, and its vastness reminding you of the endless possibilities life holds.

Chapter 16: Embracing the Power Within

The journey of a sea witch, much like the ebb and flow of the ocean, is filled with highs and lows, moments of clarity and times of ambiguity. Just as the sea is vast and its depths unknown, so is the journey into oneself. The culmination of this journey is the realization and acceptance of the power that resides within, the same power that connects you to the vast expanse of the ocean and the mysteries it holds.

The Final Voyage: Embracing Your Identity as a Sea Witch

There comes a time in every sea witch's journey when they must confront their true self, acknowledge their deep connection with the ocean, and embrace their identity wholeheartedly. This realization is akin to the first time a sailor sets out to sea, leaving the comfort of the shore behind and surrendering to the unpredictability of the ocean.

Becoming a sea witch isn't merely about performing rituals or collecting ocean treasures; it's about acknowledging the sea's influence on your life, its rhythmic pull on your spirit. Embracing your identity as a sea witch means understanding that the ocean's power, beauty, and mystery are mirrored within you. Just as the sea is ever-changing, ever-flowing, and deeply powerful, so are you.

There may have been moments of doubt, times when you questioned the authenticity of your connection to the sea. But remember, every time you've felt the call of the waves, the soothing lull of the tides, or the raw power of a storm, it was the ocean acknowledging your bond, reminding you of who you truly are.

Overcoming Challenges and Mastering Your Craft

The journey of a sea witch is not without its challenges. Just as the sea can be turbulent and unpredictable, so can the path of magic. The biggest challenge often lies within, in overcoming self-doubt, fear, and the constraints we sometimes place upon ourselves.

The external world, too, can sometimes be skeptical or even hostile to those who tread the path less taken. There will be times when your beliefs and practices might be questioned or misunderstood by others. In these moments, turn to the sea for guidance. Just as the waves relentlessly crash upon the shore, regardless of the obstacles, remain steadfast in your commitment to your craft.

Mastering the art of sea witchcraft requires dedication, patience, and constant learning. The ocean is a vast teacher, with lessons hidden in its every wave, tide, and current. Every time you engage in a ritual, every moment you spend by the shore, and with every sea treasure you collect, you're deepening your understanding and honing your skills. With time, the challenges become stepping stones, refining and strengthening your craft.

Becoming a Beacon for Others in the World of Sea Magic

As you embrace your power and master your craft, you will find yourself shining brightly in the world of sea magic. This light is not just for you but serves as a beacon for others who are drawn to the mysteries of the ocean.

Remember, the journey of every sea witch is unique, and as you have learned from the sea and those before you, there will be others who seek guidance from you. Embrace this role with humility. Share your knowledge, experiences, and the wisdom of the sea with those who seek it. By doing so, you're not only enriching the community but also ensuring that the ancient traditions, rituals, and stories of sea magic continue to flourish.

Your role as a beacon is also about leading by example. Your commitment to ethical practices, marine conservation, and respect for all oceanic beings sets a standard. It reminds and teaches others of the importance of harmonious coexistence with the ocean and all its inhabitants.

The journey of a sea witch is profound, transformative, and deeply empowering. As you embrace your inner power, remember that you're a reflection of the vast, mysterious, and beautiful ocean. With every wave you ride and every challenge you overcome, you're not only honoring the ancient traditions of sea witchery but also charting a course for future generations, ensuring that the dance with the ocean continues, forever mesmerizing and magical.